Who is that Man in the Red Suit?

The Story of How Saint Nicholas Became Santa!

Jennifer S. Goins

This book is dedicated to all who still enjoy wonder, but seek truth.

May all be moved by the love and generosity of a unique life! Blessings to you!

Love,
Jennifer

It was a cold winter day in the middle of the Christmas season. The house was all decorated and packages were already piled under the tree. Carrying her sack of books, Mary had just come down from quiet time in her room excited to see that her grandmother had finally arrived to take her to the park!

"Gran?", asked Mary.

"Yes, dear", replied Grandmother.

"I was looking at my Christmas books and don't understand why we celebrate Jesus' birthday with Santa. I love Santa! But, why does he wear only a red suit? And why is he always jolly?…".

She was just about to list more questions when Gran said, "Sit down, little one. You're old enough for me to tell you about Santa while we get you changed, brush your hair, and get ready to go outside!".

Europe

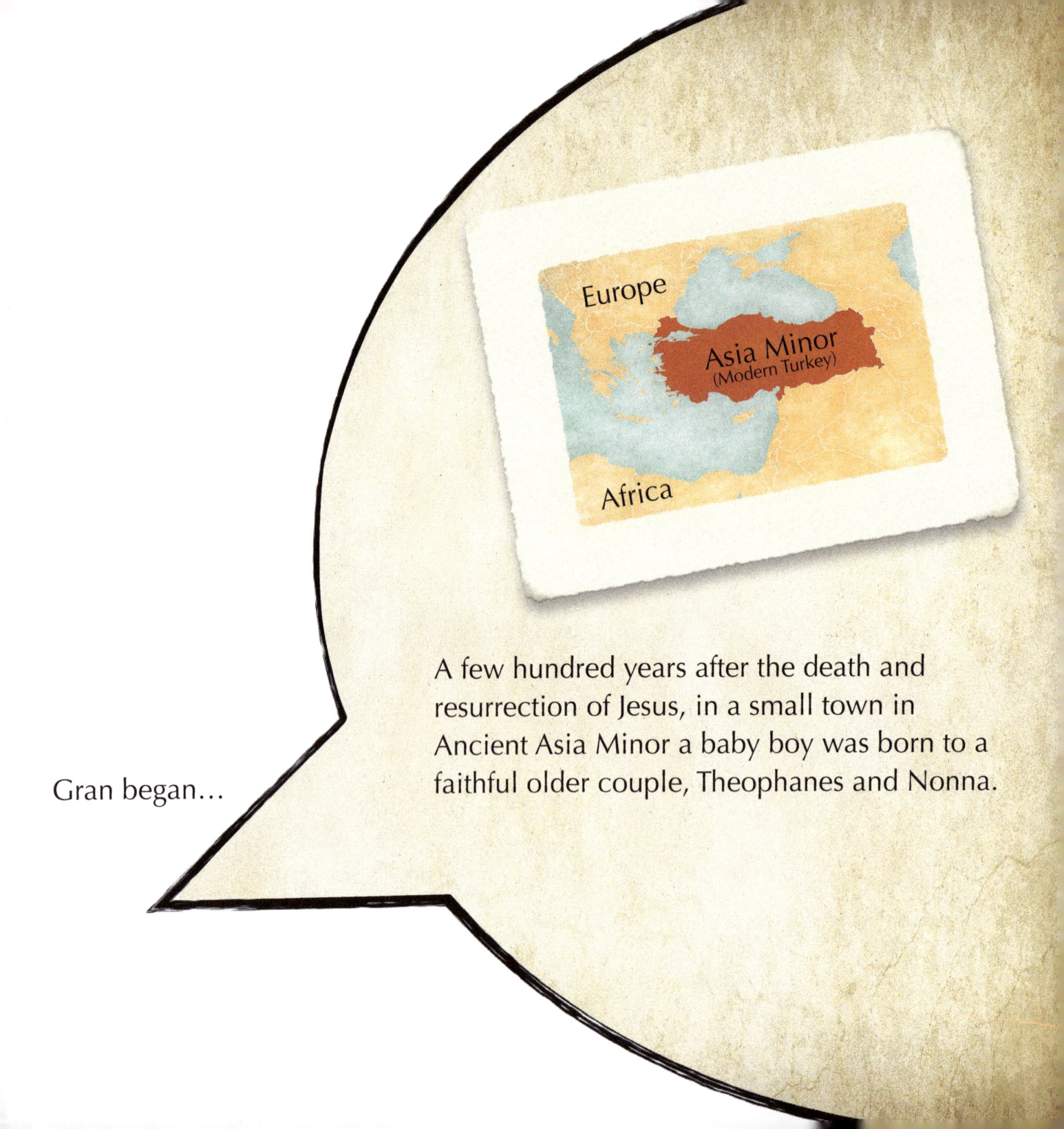

Asia Minor
(Modern Turkey)

Africa

Gran began…

A few hundred years after the death and resurrection of Jesus, in a small town in Ancient Asia Minor a baby boy was born to a faithful older couple, Theophanes and Nonna.

Much like Abraham and Sarah in the Bible, these two prayed for a child, and after many years, God answered their prayer. Believing him to be a gift from God with a special blessing on his life, they named the child Nicholas, meaning "hero of the people".

Even at a young age, Nicholas showed a special devotion to Jesus. He was known for spending much time studying the Bible and all day worshiping in church. It was clear that Nicholas was drawn to serving God! Soon enough, he entered the ministry and became ordained as a minister, preaching to and teaching the people all about God.

Sadly, while Nicholas was still a young man, his parents got very sick and passed away. They were very wealthy and left Nicholas with a large sum of money, which he generously gave to the poor, hungry, and needy in his town. He became known for taking good care of the people.

Nicholas is particularly remembered for helping a nobleman from his town who had lost his money. Creditors took the man's belongings and wanted to take away his daughters, too, if he didn't pay them what he owed. The only option left for the nobleman was to marry off his lovely daughters. In this time, the father of the bride was required to pay the groom's family a lot of money which the nobleman didn't have. Nicholas found out about this and wanted to help, but he also wanted all of the glory to go to God. So, he secretly tossed a sack of gold coins into the family's window to help the first daughter marry.

Later, he also did this for the second daughter. When it was time for the last daughter to marry, Nicholas again tossed a sack of gold coins into the window. It's said to have landed in a stocking set out to dry by the fire. When the father saw it, he ran out to investigate and found the hero was Nicholas! This later led to a tradition of secret gift giving on the anniversary of Nicholas' death, also known as Saint Nicholas' Feast Day.

At times over his life Nicholas lived as a pauper with nowhere to lay his head, but he was able to travel to the Holy Land, where Jesus lived, and he even became a Bishop! Ever humble, loving, and faithful, he confronted ungodly practices and endured persecution and imprisonment! Stories of Saint Nicholas grew throughout his region. He was known for his kindness, healing, and even miracles.

Like the Apostles and early Church Fathers, when Nicholas prayed, extraordinary things happened! People were healed, lives were saved, storms were calmed, and provisions supplied. It was evident from his life that the Spirit of God was upon him. For many years, Nicholas led his congregation. But on December 6, 343 AD, quoting from Psalm 11, "In the Lord I put my trust", Nicholas died peacefully...his life marked by his love of Jesus and others and humble, yet generous service.

After his death, stories about Nicholas' life spread and were eventually mixed with ideas from the Bible. For example, in countries like Belgium and Holland on Saint Nicholas' Feast Day, celebrated December 6, children believed he would return from heaven riding on a white horse with a book of deeds rewarding good behavior with treats and bad behavior with switches. This is similar to the book of life and the story of Christ's return in the Bible!

You see, his popularity and legend had spread from Asia Minor all the way to Western Europe, and it only continued to grow! Over the years, many churches were named in honor of Saint Nicholas. He was even named the patron saint of Russia where, because there were few horses, Saint Nicholas rode a reindeer instead of a horse!

In France, Saint Nicholas was called Pierre Noel. He was called Babbo Natalie in Italy and Sinterklass in Holland.

When Dutch settlers came to our country, America, and founded New Amsterdam in the 1600s, they brought their December traditions of the feast of Saint Nicholas with them. By this time in England, Saint Nicholas' Feast Day had been changed to a Father Christmas celebration and moved to Christmas Day. This tradition, too, was brought to America.

Like the stories of his life and the traditions honoring him, slowly over time depictions of Saint Nicholas' appearance also changed. In the 1800s his church robes were changed to a typical Dutch outfit with trunk hose by American writer Washington Irving who depicted Nicholas as an elf-ish character distributing gifts from a horse drawn wagon.

Later Reverend Clement Moore in his poem "A Visit from Saint Nicholas" changed the horses to reindeer like the stories in Sweden and Russia and described Nicholas as a cheery round gentleman with cheeks like roses.

By the late 1860s the name Saint Nicholas had evolved from the Dutch, Sinterklass, to Santa Claus. It was around this time he was illustrated by Thomas Nast as a plump jolly fellow with gnome-like features from the North Pole wearing a red suit with white fur trim.

Ultimately, it was a well-known soda company's advertisements drawn by Haddon Sundblom from the 1930s and beyond that became a sensation. They depicted Santa Claus with more realistic human characteristics and those twinkling eyes and rosy cheeks just like Reverend Moore described in his poem. This classic adaptation is still widely used today, and it's how you imagine Santa looking!

You can see how the story of Saint Nicholas grew from history into legend with modern day depictions turning him into a world-wide recognizable icon. Interestingly, over the years one aspect of Santa Claus has remained unchanged. He is known to have qualities only God Himself could have… be perfectly good, all-knowing, and unchanging. He is able to judge fairly and be everywhere! We know these are things only God can do. Just like only God can give us the greatest gift of all time!

While it's important to remember the saints, like Nicholas, who have gone before us and even admire and celebrate their acts and achievements, we must always remember that Christmas is a celebration of the birth of another real person, Jesus Christ, our Messiah, who saved us! For God so loved us that He gave His only begotten son that whoever believes in Him shall not perish but have everlasting life! This is the greatest gift and story of Christmas.

Saint Nicholas believed and spent his life living out the love of Jesus, and you can too!

...Gran explained as she helped Mary into her coat.

"Wow, Gran! That's so amazing! We not only get to celebrate Jesus at Christmas but the generosity of Saint Nicholas, too! Santa is so cool. I can't wait to share this story at school! Do you think they know?", asked Mary.

"Maybe not, sweetheart! Have fun sharing what you've learned today with them! Everyone needs hope and the love of Jesus.", Gran said.

"Gran?"

"Yes, Mary?"

"Thanks for brushing my hair!"

And off to the park they went!

Turn the page...

...to learn even more!

Christmas Symbols with Christian Meanings

Holly | Holy

Stars | The Bethlehem Star

Poinsettia | Flower of the Holy Night

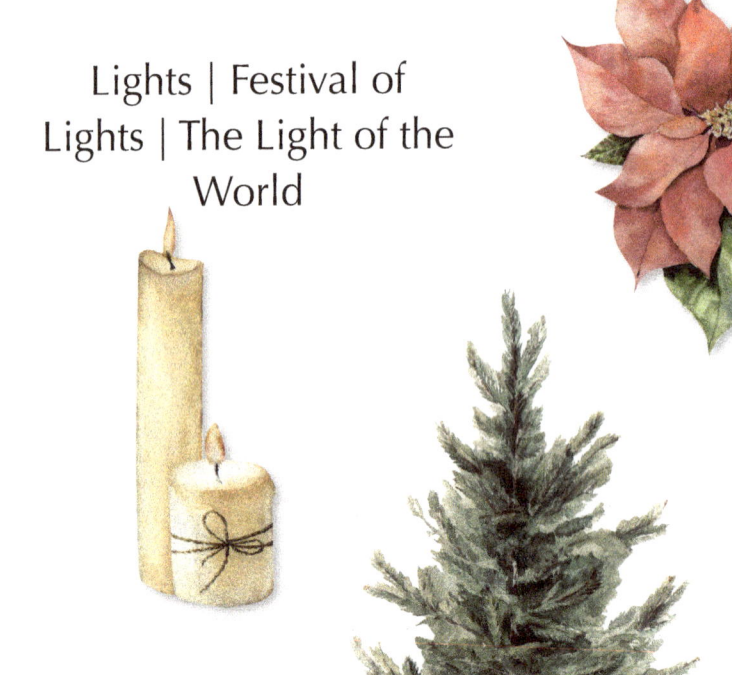

Lights | Festival of Lights | The Light of the World

Candy Cane | Red for Jesus' Blood | White for Purity

Evergreen Tree | Eternity

Round Evergreen Wreath | Eternity

Twelve Days of Christmas with Christian Meanings

During the religious persecution in England of the 1500s, doctrine was taught secretly through the hidden and symbolic meanings in songs like The Twelve Days of Christmas.

My True Love	God Himself
A Partridge in A Pear Tree	Jesus Christ on the Cross
2 Turtle Doves	Old & New Testaments
3 French Hens	Faith, Hope & Love
4 Calling Birds	Four Gospels
5 Golden Rings	Pentateuch - First 5 Books of the OT
6 Geese A-Laying	Six Days of Creation
7 Swans A-Swimming	Seven Gifts of Holy Spirit
8 Maids A-Milking	Eight Beatitudes
9 Ladies Dancing	Nine Fruits of the Holy Spirit
10 Lords A-Leaping	Ten Commandments
11 Pipers Piping	Eleven Faithful Apostles
12 Drummers Drumming	Twelves Points of the Apostles Creed

COPYRIGHT © 2022 JS Goins | Goins4Family Enterprises LLC

ISBN: 979-8-9857663-2-5 (print), ISBN: 979-8-9857663-3-2 (eBook)

No part of this publication may be reproduced or retransmitted in any form or by any means, including, but not limited to, photocopying, recording, emailing, screenshots, or by any information storage and retrieval system, without written consent from the author.

Story adapted with permission from the original work by William J. Federer, *There Really Is A Santa Claus*.

Layout and design by JS Goins. Illustrations purchased from dreamstime.com are royalty free and acceptable for commercial use. Fonts courtesy of Apple Pages. All rights reserved.

Image Credits

Santa Claus Background | ID 63194563 © Alena Fayankova | dreamstime.com
Christmas Tree with Gift Boxes | ID 163376601 | © Yuliya Derbisheva | dreamstime.com
Little Girl Reading Book | ID 237497253 © Elena Barenbaum | dreamstime.com
Map of Middle East - Turkey | ID 131611539 © Tindoarchitect | dreamstime.com
Watercolor Sketch of Series | ID49921624 © Marina Kriuchenko | dreamstime.com
Watercolor Vintage Books. ID 38373534 © Alexandra Smirnova | dreamstime.com
Old City in a Valley | ID 162958592 © Maryna Kriuchenko | dreamstime.com
Red Sack Coins (adapted) | ID 47289014 © Konstantin Gushcha | dreamstime.com
Fireplace and Holiday Socks | ID 199389875 © Yuliya Derbisheva | dreamstime.com
Saint Nicholas on Golden Background | ID 9298384 © Lindom | dreamstime.com
Sinterklaas on White Horse | ID 46388314 © Ievgen Melamud | dreamstime.com
Old Bible | ID 976547 © Cornel Krämer | dreamstime.com
Santa Claus Sleigh with Reindeer | ID 131394492 © Sergeypykhonin. | dreamstime.com
Reindeer Head | ID 68329435 © Maryia Kodun-ivanova | dreamstime.com
Horse Carriage Outdoors (adapted) | ID 76257447 © Konstantin Kostan | dreamstime.com
North Pole Sign | ID 79578979 © Ylivdesign | dreamstime.com
Vintage Santa. Illustration | ID 12478773 © Jodielee | dreamstime.com
Watercolor Santa Clause | ID 63201287 © Alena Fayankova | dreamstime.com
Watercolor Wooden Cross | ID 174324019 © Anna Kuzmina | dreamstime.com
Christmas Watercolor of Nativity | ID 227822013 © Svetlana Vorotniak | dreamstime.com
Watercolor Heart with Tree Twigs | ID 134508170 © Depiano | dreamstime.com
Old Woman with Little Girl | ID 141732705 Elena Barenbaum | dreamstime.com
Dog Year Greeting Card | ID 100320571 © Alena Fayankova | dreamstime.com
Watercolor Fir Tree | ID 110368258 © Leyasw | dreamstime.com
Watercolor Christmas Plants | ID 129464615 © Yuliya Derbisheva | dreamstime.com
Watercolor Candle | ID 101424211 © Yuliya Derbisheva | dreamstime.com
Vintage Paper | ID 16880526 © David M. Schrader | dreamstime.com
Twelve Days of Christmas | ID 17221507 © Eireanna | dreamstime.com
Twelve Days of Christmas | ID 17221494 © Eireanna | dreamstime.com
Twelve Days of Christmas | ID 17186411 © Eireanna | dreamstime.com
Twelve Days of Christmas | ID 17186398 © Eireanna | dreamstime.com
Twelve Days of Christmas | ID 17015568 © Eireanna | dreamstime.com
Twelve Days of Christmas | ID 16899720 © Eireanna | dreamstime.com
Twelve Days of Christmas | ID 16763467 © Eireanna | dreamstime.com
Twelve Days of Christmas | ID 16763421 © Eireanna | dreamstime.com
Twelve Days of Christmas | ID 16670482 © Eireanna | dreamstime.com
Twelve Days of Christmas | ID 16670676 © Eireanna | dreamstime.com
Twelve Days of Christmas | ID 16530967 © Eireanna | dreamstime.com
Twelve Days of Christmas | ID 16471695 © Eireanna | dreamstime.com
Heart Wreath | ID 33268701 © Marilyn Barbone | dreamstime.com
Watercolor Candy | ID 228673365 © Alisa Aleksandrova | dreamstime.com
Christmas Watercolor Wreath | ID 77454385 © Mika48 | dreamstime.com
Christmas Star | ID 105042110 © Sinichka | dreamstime.com

Lightning Source UK Ltd.
Milton Keynes UK
UKHW051937051222
413454UK00025B/387